You Can Draw

You Can Draw

Kenneth Jameson

Studio Vista London

Watson—Guptill Publications New York

The author and publishers would like to thank Richard Gains-borough Periodicals Ltd, 8 Wyndham Place, London, W.1., for permission to use material which first appeared in *Amateur Artist* volume 1, 1966; the author would also like to thank those students and friends whose drawings appear in these pages.

General Editor Jean Richardson
© Kenneth Jameson 1967
Published in London by Studio Vista Limited
Blue Star House, Highgate Hill, London N19
and in New York by Watson–Guptill Publications
165 West 46th Street, New York 10036
Distributed in Canada by General Publishing Co. Ltd
30 Lesmill Road, Don Mills, Toronto, Ontario
Library of Congress Catalog Card Number 68–10157
Set in Univers 8 and 9 pt.
by V. Siviter Smith & Co. Ltd, Birmingham
Printed in the Netherlands
by N. V. Grafische Industrie Haarlem

Contents

'. . . it was a canal with numerous small boats making thousands of beautiful shapes, and I think the most complete work of genius I ever saw.'

From a letter by John Constable to his friend and biographer Lesley, dated January 14th, 1832, and referring to *The Dort Packet Boat from Rotterdam, Becalmed* by J. M. W. Turner.

Introduction

The title of this book means exactly what it says: you can draw. This is certain.

What is not so certain is the precise meaning of the term 'drawing'. The academic student thinks of it quite differently from the practising 'modern' artist. Leonardo da Vinci used drawing in a different way from Paul Klee, and this book may help you to see what the differences are. Many people see drawing as a divine gift and the artist as a special person about whom there is an aura of mysticism. The Oxford Dictionary describes drawing as, 'the art of representing by line, delineation without colour or with a single colour'.

As an experiment, ask your friends to say what they understand drawing to be. You will receive surprising and differing answers. The most varied definitions will come from your artist friends, and few of them will agree with each other, or with the Oxford Dictionary.

Since 1943, I have been working with students of all ages, mostly amateur, some professional, all of whom wanted to draw. The problem common to them all was 'how to begin'. How to begin to look at the subject. How to begin on the paper. So let us take this as our point of departure.

In order to draw, the artist must be able to 'see'. This book attempts to provide the reader with a technique for training himself not merely to look but to see. For this reason, the early chapters deal with the approach to drawing, and discussion of materials and equipment is left till later. The implications of the first section, 'beginnings', can be grasped in half an hour. Once grasped, a process of self-training can then begin. As soon as your eyes are opened, your environment becomes a richer place. Every waking moment you will be able to practise 'seeing'. If your eyes are truly open, you will find yourself visually studying subject matter for possible use in drawing. It will happen all the time, on the train, in the bus, in a cafe, in the garden, at home, in the supermarket, on the beach. Every minute you spend in creative analytical looking will add to your store of visual knowledge. This in turn will add to your confidence when you engage in actual drawing. This continuous, gradual acquiring of visual 'capital', this building up of visual experience, is why any branch of art, and drawing especially, is so rewarding. One can practise it at any time, whether at, or away from, the drawing board.

This book contains reproductions of drawings by students using the approach indicated in the pages which follow. Few of them had special gifts. All of them found the thesis easy to understand, and all of them enjoyed what they did. What is of paramount importance is that they all developed in their own personal way. So, although a specific approach is suggested in this book, it is not a straight-jacket. No restriction is placed upon the development of individuality and personal sensitivity. It is not a method, it is a beginning.

1 Beginning

Adding shape to shape

One approach to drawing is to look closely at the subject, carefully to isolate the shapes, and to relate them one to another. This requires not mere looking, but *seeing*. Everybody can train himself or herself to see.

There is much more to drawing than muscular co-ordination or physical skill. It is also, and mainly, the result of careful observation. The odd thing is that there is a tendency in the inexperienced person to see only half of the subject. Let me explain what I mean.

In the photograph in fig. 1, you see a potted plant, a bottle, a book, part of a chair back, and a small ash tray. These all have their own easily recognisable shape, but these 'usual' shapes are only half of the total number of shapes. The other half are the shapes we see *between* the plant and the bottle, *between* the plant and the pot and the chair back, and so on. All the shapes are important, and to the artist the 'between' shapes are probably the more important. The illustrations in figs. 1 to 9 and the accompanying captions demonstrate one approach to 'drawing by seeing'.

Fig. 1

Fig. 2

Study the shape above. It is a 'between' shape taken from the still-life, a photograph of which you see in fig. 1. See if you can find this shape in the photograph. Do not turn to the next page until you have found it. When you have found it, you will see that the line at the top of the 'between' shape is part of a leaf; that at the upper left is part of the stalk, that at the lower left is part of the plant pot, and the line on the right is part of the chair back. The remaining short line is a canvas leaning against the wall beyond the chair. Now, turn over.

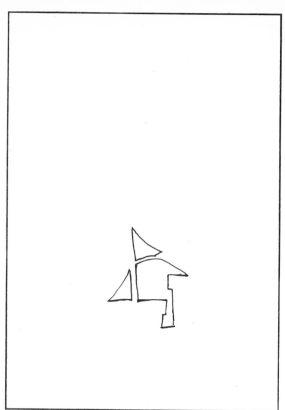

Fig. 3

Another 'between' shape has been added above the first shape. Check it in the photograph. Notice how by drawing two between shapes, we have produced the stalk of the lower right leaf. We did not actually draw that bit of stalk. It arrived by itself.

We now proceed to look all round the first between shape, and select more between shapes, so that we gradually 'grow' the drawing. In the above illustration, we have added a shape to the left of the first shape. Check with the photograph.

Fig. 4

A 'usual' shape this time, the top of the plant pot. Every new shape we add now makes the drawing more complete and easier to 'read'.

Now an easy between shape, made by the rails in the chair-back and by a corner of the canvas leaning against the wall beyond the chair.

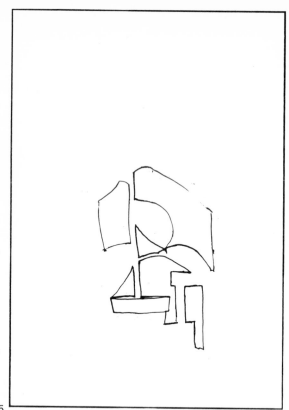

Fig. 5

A large irregular shape is added this time. It is important to notice that the vertical line on the right can only be seen by looking past the plant to the background, which in this case is the curtain. This line is a vital line, because it links the still-life elements of the group to the background.

It is time to look at the left-hand side of the subject again. Be sure you identify, in the photograph of the original, each new shape as it is added to the drawing.

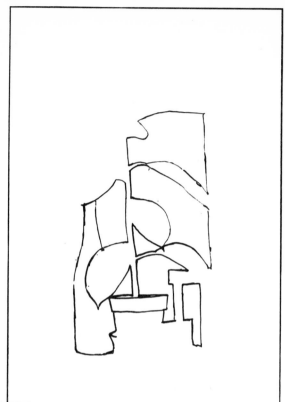

Fig. 6

A long, sweeping, but easily seen line completes the bottle, the left side of the small bowl in which the plant pot is standing, the tip of the leaf of the rubber-plant and the left side of the plant pot.

Maintaining the process of working all round the subject, we now return to the right side of the plant and work upwards. Once again, the vertical line of the background curtain plays an important part.

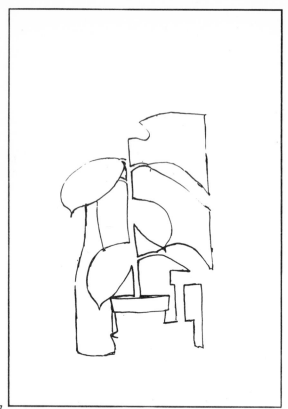

Fig. 7

The drawing is now well advanced and it is necessary to complete some more 'usual' shapes; in this case, the leaf at left above the bottle. We have now built up a firm framework.

16

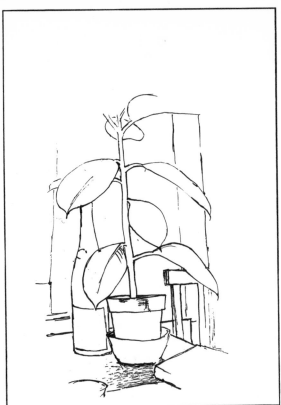

Fig. 8

This is the honeymoon stage. The drawing is safely established. It almost beckons you to add a line here, a shape there, a patch of dark in another place. The woven straw mat on the table has a textured surface. Use that to enrich your drawing. Put in those rich dark tones.

Now it is your turn. Set up an easy subject for yourself. Start with a simple group with easily seen shapes. Don't feel bound to finish your first one or two drawings all in one sitting. Select an attractive between shape to start you off, as I did. Begin by putting

Fig. 9 The drawing completed; dark tones, textures, detail, all added to give variety and interest.

that down on paper, then go and do the washing-up or a bit of gardening, and come back to the drawing later; add another shape or two, and then have another rest, and so on.

Different people work at different speeds; everyone works more quickly and confidently with practice, and as their eyes begin to open and to see more.

The first one or two attempts will be hard going. The third will be easier, and quite soon all will be plain sailing. Fig. 10 below is a first attempt by a young housewife.

Remember that you must look right through the subject from back to front, from side to side and from top to bottom if you are to see all the lines which join up to make the shapes. Carry a small sketch book in your handbag or your pocket. It is amazing what the daily five-minute drawing on the station, at the bus-stop, in the office lunch-hour, in the post office queue, will yield in progress over a short time.

In order to carry out the exercise outlined in this first series of illustrations, you don't need any mystical gift. All you require are eyes, determination and perseverance. Produce at least one drawing a day in this manner for, say, three months, and long before the end of that time you will be drawing easily and confidently and wondering why you ever thought it difficult. Progress will be slow *at first*, but it is astonishing how soon it becomes easier to *see* the shapes, and easier to put them down on paper.

Fig. 10

Subdividing the picture shape

We now continue the thesis that a large part of drawing is the seeing and relating together of shapes. But this time there is a difference. In the previous still-life example, we began by selecting an interesting between shape and continued by adding more between shapes all round the first one so that the drawing grew from the centre outwards and the final irregular outline of the finished drawing was the result of that growth.

Fig. 11

This time, we begin with a rectangle, and we proceed by sub-dividing it. The lines used to sub-divide the rectangle are selected by looking closely at the subject, this time a landscape (see fig. 12), and the first step is to decide how much of the landscape will fit satisfactorily into the rectangle on our paper. A view-finder will help the inexperienced draftsman to select the view he wants (see page 48 for details of view-finder). Fig. 12 shows the view, seen through the view-finder, which I used as a subject for the drawing discussed in this section. The photograph in fig. 11 shows the view-finder, a piece of white cardboard with a rectangular hole five inches by four, in use.

Fig. 12

Study the landscape above. With such profusion of fine detail how do we begin? The answer is simple. We begin by finding the most important shapes in the landscape and by drawing these in the rectangle of the paper. The line AA in fig. 13 illustrates in diagram form what I mean. By drawing this line from side to side, two new, smaller shapes are produced within the rectangle. But how do we find line AA? Look at the photograph of the subject and you will see that it is the far boundary line of the important foreground shape.

21

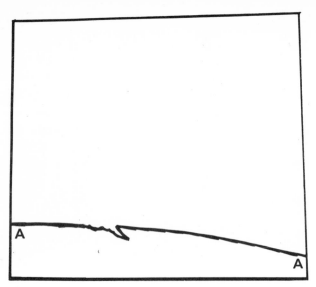

Fig. 13

Figs. 14 and 15 indicate how the process continues, until in fig. 16 all the major shapes are established.

The next stage is to take each separate major shape in turn and sub-divide it again by using the next most important lines. Complete this process all over the drawing. Then sub-divide again and again.

Drawing this kind of subject, in this way, is a matter of working from great to small; from most important to least important. It is also a matter of selection: deciding what shall be included, and what shall be left out (the fire-hydrant post for instance); where generalisations shall be made; and, by reference to the subject, what textures shall be added to enrich the drawing, what tones of light and dark.

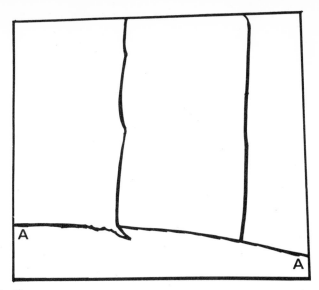

Fig. 14

The trunks of the two main trees provide the next most important lines: two irregular verticals which join AA to the top line of the rectangle. As you will see in the figure above, these produce four major shapes. These three lines are the 'master lines' of the drawing. Judge the shapes which these produce correctly, state the lines firmly and connect them to the outlines of the rectangle, and your 'composition' will be established.

Take care to note the difference in width of the vertical shapes.

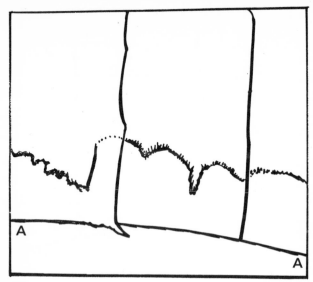

Fig. 15

The next line is subtle and yet powerful. If you cannot easily see it in the photograph of the landscape subject, close one eye completely and nearly close the other. The line will then become readable as a line. It is a 'resultant' line, and is produced by the tips of literally thousands of twigs which form the outline of the mass of trees in the middle distance.

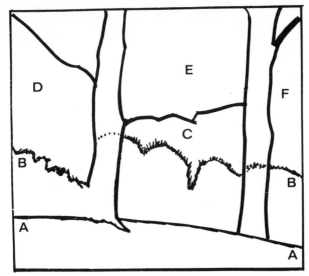

Fig. 16

The trunk shapes are completed and two large branches added. All the major shapes are now established in outline. Figs. 13 to 16 are diagrams only, to show the major shapes in the subject. They are printed in heavy line for clarity in reproduction. If you were starting this drawing from the beginning, you would set up the same framework, but in very fine lines. The next stage, fig. 17, shows just such a fine line framework on to which shading or tone has been added by using the flat side of a black grease crayon. The tones in the trunks were added with soft lead-pencil.

Fig. 17

The addition of the branch linking the two main trees creates two more shapes: E and C. Starting from now, the camera will record each stage of this drawing until it is completed and frequent reference will be made to the shapes C, D, E and F in the last of the diagramatic drawings, i.e., fig. 16.

26

Fig. 18

Let us take E and C together and consider them to be one single shape. Now, study this area in the photograph of the subject. Sort out, and draw in, the most important big branches and the trunks of the smaller trees which you can see in this shape. Take no notice of minor twigs and branches at this stage.

The same procedure is now carried out in shape D. By comparing my version with the original, see whether you agree with me about the most important branches of the main tree (on the left) and the shapes of the more distant trunks in this area. By 'most important' branches and trunks, I mean those which are most obvious, which attract your eye most strongly.

27

Fig. 19

Fig. 20

28

Fig. 21

The same process is again applied to shape F. It will be very much worth your while really to study fig. 19 and to compare it critically with the original. Don't take everything I say on trust; check me, and see if you agree with my selection of the main elements of the subject. I hope that before very long you will be making just such a drawing as this entirely under your own steam. You must train yourself to be critical of everything you draw; begin that training now by practising on my drawing.

We now reach the really enjoyable part of the drawing. Everything is now sorted out and is easy to see. What before was a confusing mass of detail, difficult to differentiate, is now a profusion of lines, textures and tones. We can choose what we will from these, and use them to enrich the major and minor shapes within the drawing. In the illustrations opposite and above the main shapes have been enriched in this way.

Fig. 22

Further general enrichment, especially of shapes D and F. When those have been dealt with, let us see what else must be added to give a feeling of completeness and harmony to the drawing: a hazy texture of twigs top left and on the tops of the minor trees; a strengthening of the dark tone of the mass of middle-distance trees; a merging together of some of the detail at bottom right; look more closely at the texture of the bark on the left-hand main tree. This for me is the most satisfying part of the work, this 'pulling it together' as it is called.

Fig. 23 The completed drawing.

Some readers may prefer to restrict themselves to one medium. I enjoy using a variety of drawing materials all in one drawing.

One word of caution: it is easy to be tempted to go on and on drawing, so remember that more work is spoilt by drawing too much than by drawing too little. Don't over do it. The media used in this drawing were: lead pencil, heavy grade; felt-tip marker pen; fibre-tipped pen; ball-point pen; black grease crayon, large size.

Now, make a view-finder and go and find a landscape subject which has strong, easily-seeable shapes.

Footnote
It would have been possible to approach this landscape drawing by using the 'adding' system we used for the still-life subject. You could try this. Such an exercise would help you to decide which is the better method, *for you.*

Composing around a vertical axis

The first of these 'Beginning' sections showed an approach to drawing involving the selection of a central shape and then the adding of other observed shapes round the first.

The second indicated a different but related approach: that of taking elements from an observed landscape and using these to break down the rectangle of the paper into its component related shapes.

This section offers another method of composing and developing a drawing. Basically it is the arrangement of the major parts of the composition (see fig. 24) on either side of a vertical axis. In this case, the vertical axis is an irregular, isolated stump of break-water on the beach, surrounded by pebbles, driftwoods and shells, and so on. As you will see, it stretches from very near the bottom of the paper to the top. Its use in determining the com-position of the drawing is rather like that of a calibrated scale used for measuring. It is visually and mathematically easy to judge the points where the horizontal lines of the composition pass behind the vertical and the proportions of the distances between these points (fig. 25). Having found and established these points on the vertical, it is then a simple matter to look at the subject and build the shapes related to the vertical on either side of it.

A little imagination will show how the vertical-axis principle can operate when other different types of subject are being attempted. In landscape, the vertical-axis can be, perhaps, the trunk of a tall tree. In a seascape, it could be the mast of a boat. A tall lamp standard will serve when a 'city-scape' is the subject, and pylons or cranes in industrial subjects.

We have already looked quite closely at two differing approaches to drawing. Before we embark upon a third, we must think for a moment about what prompts us to draw in the first place.

Significant drawing cannot come into being unless the artist has been stimulated to draw. The artist must be 'sparked off' by something he experiences. To draw for the sake of drawing, or from a vague sense of wanting to draw, will produce work which is little better than 'knitting'. On the other hand, to be so stimulated as to be compelled to set down in graphic terms, on paper, some-thing about a strong personal experience will produce meaningful drawing. This applies whether the draftsman is amateur or professional.

The objects which make up this third subject were all found

32

during a walk along the beach. Each one attracted my attention because of some special quality it possesses: patterns in the pebbles, textures in the driftwoods, sea-worn forms, subtle colour. Each one provided me with its own peculiar visual or tactile experience. I am fascinated by the beach, and for this reason I am sensitive to everything about it. The experiences it provides are so strong that I am stimulated to draw and so to try to capture some of the magic.

Try the following simple exercise. Walk along the beach or river bank and search for dark pebbles with light veining. They can be any size. Small ones are more convenient, especially if you have a long walk home! Wash them and lay them on a sheet of grey paper. Examine them closely, with a magnifying glass if they are very small, then draw them, paying special attention to the pattern made by the contrast of the dark and light. It helps if you simplify the pattern; and if you emphasise it.

Different people have their own particular interests. An artist colleague of mine produced a series of fascinating works based on 'junk-yards'. What are your special interests? They may well produce good subject matter for drawing. Whatever else you do, don't 'knit'. You will *know* when you find subject matter which really moves you to draw.

Fig. 24

It is worth stressing that the subject we are going to study together now is concerned with shape, form, texture, pattern, tone, and line, for their own sakes. These are abstract qualities; and in this drawing these abstract qualities are perhaps even more significant than the objects depicted.

34

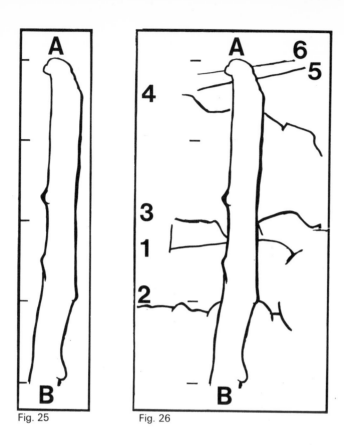

Fig. 25   Fig. 26

The irregular vertical is set up (fig. 25). The five points between A and B indicate four convenient comparative distances. Visualise these in imagination while looking at the subject on the previous page. Keep these in mind while deciding the next step.

Still looking at the subject, find the irregular horizontal lines 1 2, 3, 4, 5, 6, which pass behind the vertical. These horizontals are composite lines. Line 2, for instance, is produced, from left to right, by parts of a pebble, a shell, another pebble, an erroded brick, sand and the fisherman's float.

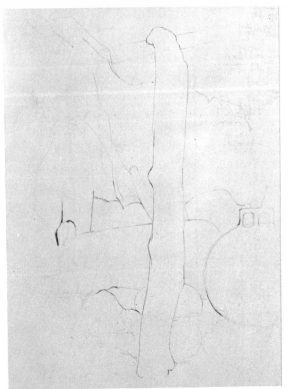

Fig. 27

The two figures on the previous page were diagrammatic. Now let us begin the drawing proper. The first thing is to establish the irregular vertical and the horizontals which pass behind it. We now have a 'skeleton' into which we can draw. It is comparatively easy to see lines which we can use to complete the shapes already partially drawn. They are closely related to each other and to the vertical. The vertical form is the dominant feature of the composition.

Fig. 28

I shall proceed now, with the camera watching over my shoulder, to add some of the tones. The drawing needs 'support'. I like to distribute the darks right across the drawing as soon as possible, so as to keep a balance as the work progresses. Note that the darks are shapes in their own right.

Fig. 29

In this illustration we continue the process of developing the pattern of darks and half-tones. Note particularly how the more intricate sections are simplified, the large driftwood especially. The main shape is taken, the detail contained in that shape is discarded. This is abstraction in its simplest form.

Fig. 30

We begin now to look more closely at the textures of the various objects. I was impelled to make this drawing by these textural qualities. Seashore objects are to me magical and evocative. Their forms are strange, their patterns are timeless and universal.

Fig. 31

Pattern: one of the most fascinating aspects of this kind of
subject. Look at the three patterned pebbles in the foreground.
Note how dramatically and clearly the shape of the pebble is
divided up into subsidiary related shapes by the contrast of light
and dark.

Fig. 32

Still looking for shapes within shapes and textures within shapes
we find exquisite little details on the razor-shell and the small
twig of heather-root. They are minute in themselves, yet they add
subtle, but telling, enrichment to the total effect.

Fig. 33

The tone in the centre of the drawing, on the centre plank of driftwood, is darkened. The tone generally is darkened. The drawing is unified by laying a broad, loose 'cross-hatching' right across it (see page 57 for cross-hatching). The less important pebbles are added round the perimeter.

Fig. 34

The final stage, entailing the addition of touches of textures of sand and the delicate tracery of the sea-worn root at bottom right. See how 'telling' this is. The last modification was that of again reducing the contrast of tones by cross-hatching right across the drawing.

On the following two pages you will see two further examples of the vertical axis in use.

Fig. 35   Fig. 36

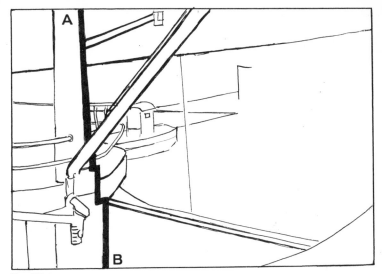

Fig. 37

Fig. 38

45

Making it look right

Some amateur artists are haunted by the idea that their work does not 'look right'. When pressed to say what they mean by 'right', their explanation, usually, is that it does not look 'like' the subject. If pressed further, it becomes clear that this particular inhibition is the result of the erroneous belief that art is primarily concerned with 'imitation'. Of course it is not. It is concerned with the use of art media for the expression and communication of aesthetic experience. This may not involve imitation of any kind.

In drawing, which is our present concern, this lack of 'rightness' is nearly always attributed to inability to cope with the intricacies of 'perspective'. What a pity perspective ever strayed from the field of science and optics, where it belongs, to the sphere of artistic expression where it does not. It is significant that very few colleges of art now teach perspective as such. If inability to manage perspective threatens to stop you drawing, then abandon perspective. If, on the other hand, you really *need* a way of dealing with it, because that is part of what you want to express, there is no problem. If you have absorbed the three previous sections, you already possess a built-in solution.

Once again, it is a matter of shapes; this time relating the shapes, and particularly the lines which define these shapes, to the edge of the view-finder; and because in the early stages this simple device is such an invaluable aid, we must pause for a moment and consider it.

A view-finder is nothing more than a rectangular hole cut in any convenient material, cardboard, plastic, etc. A 35 mm slide

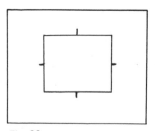 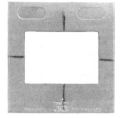

Fig. 39

Fig. 40

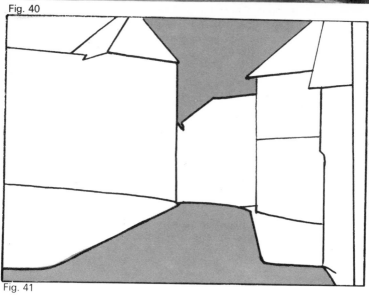
Fig. 41

47

mount makes a very convenient small one to carry in a ticket-pocket or handbag. The rectangular hole can be any proportion to suit your taste. I find a proportion of 4 : 5 is a good shape. You will decide, in the light of practice, whether you prefer a squarish shape or a longer thinner proportion. In any event the shape of the rectangle in the view-finder is not so important as the function of the view-finder. This function is two-fold. First, it isolates that bit of your environment which has captured your attention and which you have decided to use as subject matter. In other words, it cuts out the confusing detail which presses in from all sides surrounding your subject. It makes it easier for you to see *your* bit. Secondly, the rectangle provides two lines vertical in direction and two lines horizontal in direction, and against these it is easy to see the direction of the lines of your subject. Look at fig. 40. This is what I saw through my view-finder at Ingrandes, in the Loire valley in France. Study it. As the lines of the curbstones go towards the top of the view-finder, do they lean to the left or to the right? If these lines were continued down to the bottom edge, what sort of angles would they make; 45°, 50°, 80°? And yet why go to all this trouble? Look back for a moment to fig. 2 on page 11. If you succeeded in picking out that small shape in that still-life subject, you will certainly have no difficulty in picking out and drawing the shape of the road in the Ingrandes picture.

The thing to remember is if you get that shape right, and the other shapes right, the drawing will look right; the perspective will be right. Now look at the rest of the shapes in fig. 40 and relate them to the road shape, taking the large shapes first. The sky shape is the one I found most interesting and most helpful to continue with. Now build the small shapes into the big shapes.

One more very important point. When using the view-finder, the horizontals and verticals of the hole through which you look govern your judgement of angles and lines and your seeing of shapes. When making a drawing using a view-finder to view the subject, the horizontals and verticals of the edges of your paper, or your sketch book, govern the angle at which you draw your line and form parts of the shapes you are transferring from your view-finder to the paper. In other words, the rectangle in which you draw on the paper and the view-finder rectangle through which you look are really one and the same; you should think of them as the same, or at least think of them as corresponding exactly.

Fig. 42

Of course, as time goes on, you will find it less and less
necessary to use the actual view-finder because you will eventu-
ally find yourself putting imaginary view-finders round everything you look at.

Take care of the *shapes* and the *perspective* will take care of
itself.

Fig. 43

Automatic, automotive drawing

All the four previous sections have dealt with ways of beginning to draw which involve the artist in looking outwards at the visible world; in analysing, computing, composing, judging and arranging. This is only half the story. Many artists draw upon their own inner imaginings for subject matter. You have only to look at the work of William Blake to see what I mean.

I once asked a three-year-old girl what she was drawing. 'I don't know' she replied, 'I haven't finished it yet'. This was not a silly answer. It was her way of saying that if she put the pen or pencil on the paper, and moved it about, it made marks; and that if she continued the process, gradually something recognisable as a shape would appear amongst the dots and scribbles. In other words, she drew first, and found something in her drawing afterwards. This is in fact a very common form of drawing which every reader of this book has practised at some time or another. I mean the 'doodle' on an odd envelope, on the scrap-pad at the committee meeting, on the blotter while telephoning. This doodling is automatic or automotive. It is produced by a combination of the whim of the eye, a primitive feeling for pattern, and a sort of sensuous, rhythmical, muscular enjoyment of sliding the ball-point or the soft lead-pencil smoothly over the surface of the paper. I wonder whether you have ever sat down and deliberately, consciously, created a doodle. If you haven't, try it now. Then go and find reproductions of works by Joan Miró and of drawings by Paul Klee. There is inspired doodling for you; and I mean no disrespect to either artist.

Henry Moore speaks of 'drawing as a means of generating ideas'. Drawing means drawing. It does not often mean imitating. It means creating. It means exploring. It means finding. It means imagining. In this kind of expression there are no rules. You are master of the situation. There is nothing to stop you 'creating'. You are free from any kind of inhibition.

2 Study

Discovery and development

'Beginnings' to start you off, now 'study' to consolidate.

Open exhibitions usually include the work of both professional and amateur artists, and it is often difficult to see which is which; but go to their studios and differences will be much more apparent. I can imagine wry comments at the mention of 'studios' by all those industrious amateurs who have to manage on the

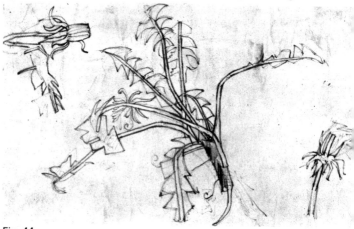

Fig. 44

draining board in the kitchen or on the window-sill in the spare bedroom. On second thoughts, one recalls the palatial studios of some wealthy amateurs compared with the bare boards and single rooms of some professionals, so perhaps it would be more realistic to say go to the place where the artist, amateur or professional, works and look at the *way* he works. It is here that the difference lies. The professional works all the time, or the majority of the time. In his studio evidence of activity will be everywhere, but he is not continuously engaged on one piece of work for an exhibition or one work for a client. Specific work of this kind may occupy as little as fifty per cent of his time. The other fifty per cent is likely to be spent in study, whether he be Leonardo in his notebooks, Turner in his *Liber Studiorum,* Henry Moore in his *Shelter Sketchbooks,* or any art student in any college of art progressing through his professional training as an artist.

By study I mean visual exploration, visual analysis, close observation, abstraction, extraction, and the noting down in any medium of the discoveries made by these processes in sketch form. A series of well filled sketch books is likely to indicate a mature or maturing artist. Study is the aesthetic food which ensures the growth and development of the artist. Perhaps the most valuable aspect of study is that it makes the artist more and more sensitive to his surroundings and to his own reactions to those surroundings.

The five subheadings of the previous chapter aim to provide the reader with ways of beginning to see, to analyse, to generate ideas, and to set down subject matter. This section on study follows on logically. Study is the way of developing from the 'beginnings' stage. We shall now deal more fully with terms already used in chapter 1 such as form, texture, tone, pattern. The serious student must know about these aspects of drawing. Study is the way he can discover and experience them for himself, and by persistent study the amateur can achieve a professional standard.

Form

In chapter one a good deal has been written about 'shape', and this really implies two dimensions. Many draftsmen are satisfied with a flat, two-dimensional approach. Some, on the other hand, will want to develop methods of expressing depth, distance, solidity, three-dimensional shape, form. This is a complex matter. For the keen amateur it provides a wide area of further study which will add new drawing technique to that which he has gained so far. So let us begin by concentrating our attention upon what is the more obvious aspect of the subject; I mean the expression of solid form.

Figs. 45a and 45b

There are various ways of doing this; we will consider two.

1. The use of drawing technique to show the three-dimensional structure of an object.

2. The use of drawing technique to express the form of an object as revealed by the play of light across its surfaces.

Take two basic forms, the cube and the cylinder; figs. 45a and 46a show the expression of the structural form in line. Figs. 45b and 46b show the expression of the form as revealed by light.

Now experiment for yourself with cones, ovoids, cuboids, rhomboids, pyramids, etc. And before you exclaim, 'shades of Methuselah, cones and cubes went out with the Ark!!', let me say I am not advocating that you should go on and on drawing cubes and tetrahedrons and the rest. I *am* advocating that you should make yourself familiar with fundamental forms. It was Cézanne who said all nature can be reduced to four or five basic,

Figs. 46a and 46b

Fig. 47   Fig. 48

solid, geometrical forms. So remember that these are the basic forms we find in our natural and man-made environment. Look round you, now, and you will see that I am right. After all, what is a country cottage but a cuboid form with a prism or a pyramid on top. What is a tree but a cylinder with an irregular ovoid on top. What is a human figure but an assembly of modified cylinders, cones, hemispheres and a few other forms.

In due course you may want to try your hand at life-drawing. The nude human body is perhaps the most complex of all forms, and as such is a challenge to any draftsman. Professional models are expensive. It is more economical to join a local life-drawing class where the expense of the model's fee is shared equally among all the students, and where, in addition, you will probably get help from a qualified instructor.

Practice will quickly enable you to make simple forms look solid. As soon as you have mastered this stage, turn your attention to making all your subjects look solid.

56

Tone

Tone is all those variations between extreme light and extreme dark, and in drawing it is produced by 'shading' of various kinds (see fig. 49). There are no rules. All that matters is that you should achieve the effect you want. You can use dots, lines, cross-hatching (fig. 50), wash (fig. 51), random scribble or any other method you can invent. You will decide which looks best and which gives you the result you want.

Fig. 49

Fig. 50

The rendering of tone is an indispensible part of the draftsman's technique. With it he can:
1. produce the illusion of light
2. help to define the form in his drawing
3. represent 'local colour'. In other words, give the tonal equivalent of, for instance, the green of the grass as compared with the darker green of tree foliage.

A theme for study could be a series of drawings of a simple form, say a tree trunk. The exercise could consist of:
1. drawing the trunk under different intensities of light
2. rendering the tone with as many different media as you can think of
3. matching the 'local colour' in the tree trunk.
Note how the tone changes gradually on a curved form and suddenly on a sharp-edged form. (See figs. 45b and 46b).

Make a series of studies of the effects of light in monochrome (or one colour). This will force you to analyse tone. Note how in fig. 52 the tone representing the cast shadow on the road also defines the form of the rounded surface of the road.

If you find difficulty in distinguishing between 'near' tones, shut one eye and nearly close the other and then look again. You will find it much easier because then the tones separate themselves out more definitely.

Light, tone and form, are closely linked.

Fig. 51

Fig. 52

Pattern

Since time immemorial artists, cavemen, ancient Egyptians, Greeks, whatever their medium, have turned to nature for inspiration when creating patterns. The wood and stone carvers, the illuminators, the painters of the middle ages used leaf, flower, animal and human forms in their decorative arts. So too do artists today. Nature is a rich storehouse for the artist to draw upon. Every serious student will, *must*, study pattern in nature. Once you begin to look at patterns in pebbles, in animal markings, in flower forms, leaf formations, sea forms, graining in wood, a new world will open before your eyes. Once you begin to see natural pattern, a visit to the botanical gardens or a walk along the beach becomes a tingling, vital experience.

Have you ever really looked at the interior of a cauliflower, cut horizontally, cut vertically; at an orange, a tomato, or a pomegranate cut in half; or looked through a view-finder at the rhythmical sweep of the branches of a mature horse-chestnut tree in winter; the list is endless. Drawing pattern in nature means studying pattern in nature: it means seeking out pattern in nature in order to draw it. Every drawing you make enriches your mental store of pattern; a store upon which you can draw at will and when needed to enrich your drawings.

Study of pattern begets sensitivity to pattern. This kind of sensitivity will develop your visual appreciation of your environment, provide standards of judgment, and make you a richer person. For this reason alone a study of pattern in nature is more than worthwhile.

Fig. 53

Texture

Texture in its commonest sense, in the graphic and plastic arts at any rate, has to do with the appearance of surfaces and their tactile quality. The mature painter and draftsman will extract every bit of expressive quality from the textures in the surfaces he represents and the surfaces he creates. Think for a moment of a Van Gogh painting, of the late period, of a corn-field. Then think of a drawing of the same subject by the same artist. In the first you will certainly see a good example of texture built up by paint. In the second you will see that the artist has used short pen strokes, massed together as a drawn texture, to express the idea of stubble or corn stalks. It must be true to say that Van Gogh, knowing the rich effect such textures produce in a painting or drawing, deliberately chose subjects which enabled him to use such textures.

Try setting up a still life subject composed entirely of objects which appeal strongly to you because of their texture. Then reinforce this exercise by making drawings after close study of everyday textures which may so far have escaped your notice. Use a magnifying glass if necessary, and a view-finder.

The illustrations in figs. 54 to 58 are typical texture studies of two aspects of trees, i.e., foliage and bark. Try similar exercises for yourself. Then turn your attention to brick walls, stone walls, rocks, ploughed fields, stubble fields, clouds, roofs, clothing materials, human hair textures, street and road surfaces; the list is literally endless.

Study of textures will not only provide understanding of their use to enrich drawings and paintings, it will also lead you to a new awareness of natural and man-made objects. As with pattern, so with texture; you are likely to become more sensitive to your environment and everything in it. The more sensitive the artist is to his environment, the more he experiences of it. The more vivid his experiences, the more expressive his drawings and paintings will be.

Persistent study is the key to creative sensitivity. The more knowledge we can amass through experience, the better artists we shall be.

Figs. 54, 55, 56

Figs. 57, 58

Working to a theme

In the beginning students tend to work over a wide area of subject matter; then gradually they find themselves drawn towards certain themes. General study provides overall development of skill and sensibility; study to a theme produces experience in depth. Think of some obvious cases. Van Gogh's persistent theme was sunlight and its effect on the hot landscape of France. In the early days of John Bratby meal-table subjects produced a remarkable series of still-life paintings. Pierre Bonnard's recurrent theme was his wife in the bath.

The corollary of this is that if you make enough studies over a wide area, sooner or later you will find your own personal interests. Your special themes will emerge and will claim more of your artistic study-time. In other words, you will find your own personal artistic identity. This is a process you cannot hurry, and it is the only way to become an artist. It is fallacious to think that if one takes lessons and 'learns' to paint still-life, or portrait, or landscape, one will then automatically become an artist. It is fatuous to draw or paint a subject which somebody else has arranged for you if you have no interest in it. It is useless to allow other people to suggest subjects for you to draw. It is a waste of time for you to say to yourself, 'everybody else draws still-life, so I'd better draw still-life'. You don't choose your subject matter; your subject matter chooses you. Let me explain what I mean. You see something. It attracts your attention. You become fascinated by it. You feel you *must* draw it. If you feel excited enough about your subject, your drawing will communicate your excitement to the viewer. This is artistic expression. It grows out of experience, as a result of study, and looking, and involvement with environment.

I know a woman painter who is constantly attracted by the theme of birds. This arises out of her deep interest in this form of nature. Now search into your own interests and find a theme; the beach, the woods, trees, the markings on tree-trunks, churches, steeples, fossils, forms seen through a microscope, rock-forms, pattern, texture, folk-design. The choice is as wide as the sum of man's experience.

Museum study

Under the general heading of 'study' mention must be made of the academic exercise known as 'museum study'. Go into any major art gallery or museum during term time and you will almost certainly find earnest art students, sketch-book in hand, busily making copies and details from the works of the masters, drawing studies of decorative chasing in armour, of medieval motifs from costume, and the rest. This sort of activity is standard practice for art students. It is a way of coming to grips with the mind of the Master, or perhaps with some aspect of art and craft or of the history of art and craft. The practice cannot be too highly recommended, whether your interest lies in the history and appreciation of art, or whether you are making a study of a craft. To the student with a special interest in drawing, a first-hand study of the drawings of the Old Masters is a revealing experience.

If you are interested in a craft such as pottery, sculpture, theatre design, dress design, keep study-notebooks in which you can compile a sketch-record of design details related to your particular medium, whether it be ideas culled from the work of great practitioners of the past or present, or studies from nature of material likely to be useable in future work.

The term 'study' is also used to mean preliminary jottings of ideas for major works. Every serious student should note down all his ideas and gradually build up a collection of these 'studies'. Keep for future reference and possible development all your 'try-outs', all your sketch notes and working drawings.

Drawings produced as the result of painstaking and devoted museum study are creative capital in the artistic bank. Next time you go to an art gallery, museum, or zoological gardens etc., remember to take your sketch book.

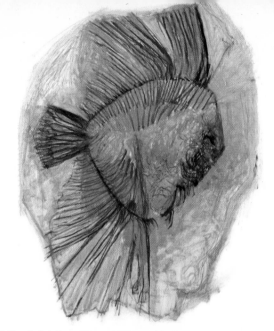

Fig. 59 Fossil fish from Natural History Museum. Pastel. Size: 20″ × 15″.

Fig. 60 Moulded dish decorated; slip and sgraffito. Size: 14″.

The drawn line

To a good many people the term drawing immediately conjures up the mental image of an H.B. lead-pencil, whereas in fact any implement capable of making a line can be used for drawing. Lines can be cut in wood, lino, or metal. They can be bitten out of metal with acid, they can be cut in glass with a diamond or a carborundum wheel. Lines can be drawn with chalks, brushes and ink, brushes and paint; with pens of all descriptions. Lines can be printed with screens; or sewn with cotton and a sewing machine (fig. 61). Lines can be produced by wax resist methods. A needle sharp point can be used to scratch through a black coating superimposed on a white ground thus revealing the white beneath (scraperboard or scratchboard). One could enumerate many more mediums: charcoal, grease-crayon, pastel, redhot poker-work. Indians draw by trailing streams of coloured sand from their hands. Confectioners draw with icing sugar syringes. Potters draw with slip-trailers (fig. 62).

I am labouring this point because it is so important to stress that drawing is a universal activity. From the earliest age, long before they can talk, very young children are able to some extent

Fig. 61

to communicate through drawing; and whether or not they communicate, they draw. Some form of drawing is used by everybody. It is odd that, in spite of its universality, drawing is hedged around by conventions and formulas.

I urge you not to be conventional, but to look for your own formula. Experiment with as many different media as possible; invent new media for yourself; vary the scale of your drawings and mix your media, so that you can find the linear tool which best suits your needs.

Fig. 62 Drawing with a slip trailer—the potter's clay equivalent of the confectioner's icing-sugar technique.

Fig. 63 *The Haunted House* This drawing was motivated in the first place by curiosity to see what a Welsh farm-house, reputed to be haunted, looked like. It was carried out in a mixture of media. Amongst these were wax resist; the white branches in the hedge on the left; a pen made from a dead

hollow stem plucked from the hedge; a stick pen, a hog-hair (bristle) brush and sepia wash. Size of original drawing: 30″ × 22″ on cartridge (drawing) paper.

3 Drawing in line and wash

The term 'wash' has been used though not defined in an earlier section of this book. It means simply a layer of paint. A water-colour wash is a layer of watercolour paint, and this, or a wash of ink, or dilute ink, is the sort of wash most frequently used in conjunction with drawing.

If a drawing is carried out in steel pen, ball-point pen, reed pen or indeed any medium using liquid ink, an effective wash can be produced by making a pen stroke and then, with a brush loaded with water, brushing across and around the drawn line while it is still wet. By so doing the brush carries some of the ink with it and tints, or adds a tone, to the surrounding area of paper.

If you want to lay an even wash over the whole paper surface, either before or after the drawing is done, the procedure is as follows.

Fig. 64

72

Tilt the drawing board or sketch book to an angle of, say, twenty-five degrees. Mix more wash than you need. Charge the watercolour brush, which should be not less than size eight, and run a continuous stroke across the page from side to side. Dip again and run another continuous stroke just touching the one above. There will be a surplus of liquid and this will flow downwards to the lower edge because of the tilt of the working surface. Working quickly, continue to dip and work across the paper from side to side, just touching the line above each time. Maintain a plentiful flow of wash all the time so that it will always run down by gravity. Continue until you reach the bottom of the paper. Pinch the brush dry and lift off the surplus liquid by touching the dry bristles to the excess wash. Keep the work surface in the sloping position until it is dry to avoid blemishing the lower edge by 'runback'. With practice this process will produce a flat, even wash. One word of caution. Do not be tempted to make more than one stroke with each charging of the brush, even if there appears to be a considerable excess of wash. Success in producing an even wash depends upon achieving a state of luxurious fluidity.

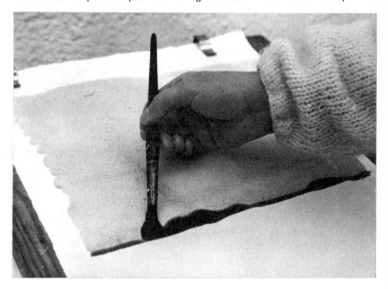

Fig. 65

Some subjects call for the use of a 'broken' wash. This is a wash with a deliberately contrived patchy or irregular appearance. There is no set way of achieving this. It is normally produced with a brush less heavily loaded, and the strokes may be applied in any or all directions, in small areas, singly or superimposed.

A single wash is a quick and effective way of adding a tone over a wide area of drawing.

The word enrichment has been used a good deal in earlier sections. Washes can be used for enriching drawings by the addition of colour (see figs. 89, 91 and 92).

If the aim of the artist is to produce a drawing, he must ensure that the wash, whether it be colour or monochrome, is transparent, so that it does not obscure the line of the drawing.

A wide range of effects can be achieved by experimenting with ink, pencil, charcoal, pastel and the rest and wet wash. An adventurous mixing of media produces surprises and variety, and makes for flexibility of expression.

Fig. 66 This drawing of corn stooks shows the use of wash, and how texture can be produced by scrubbing and stippling with an almost dry brush.

74

4 Drawing implements

In the previous section we have been considering some of the more unconventional ways of drawing. Let us now look at the more conventional media. They divide into two main groups, solid media and liquid media.

The first group includes:

chalks	pastels, sanguine, white chalk, conté
crayons	oil pastels, wax (large and small)
pencils	lead, charcoal, wax, conté, watercolour pencils, sanguine

The second group includes:

pens	steel nib, fountain pen, ball-point, fibre-point, felt-tipped, reed pen, bamboo pen, stick pen, quill pen
brush	brush and ink, brush and paint, mop

Do not be content until you have tried all these media. In particular, try out, experiment with, and invent new types of home-made pens and other drawing implements. From the list given above, felt-tipped pens, reed pens, bamboo pens, stick pens, and mops can all be made at home for little or no cost.

If you have a studio or working space where you can experiment without fear of making a mess, try pinning a large sheet of paper to the wall. Then make a felt-tip pen by splitting the end of a bamboo cane and inserting a one inch by two inches piece of thick felt (fig. 67). Now try making a drawing with the bamboo-felt-pen held at arm's length. Then try smaller drawings with smaller, home-made, felt-tipped pens.

Next time you go for a walk, if your way takes you near a reed bed pull up a few reeds and use them to make pens. It is the simplest job in the world. Fig. 68 shows you how to do it. Try a large scale drawing with your reed pen. Van Gogh was fond of

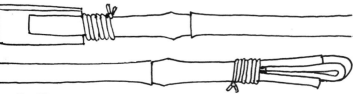

Fig. 67

drawing with this implement. Alternatively a gardening shop usually supplies quarter-inch bamboo canes suitable for making bamboo pens, which are made in the same way as reed pens. They are, really, a more durable version of the reed pen and are valuable for use in schools where wear and tear on materials is usually considerable. If reeds or bamboos are not available, Michelmas Daisy or cow-parsley stems or any weed or flower with a fairly rigid stem would be just as good. In fact any dead and dry hollow stem will do. See what you can find in the garden or the local park.

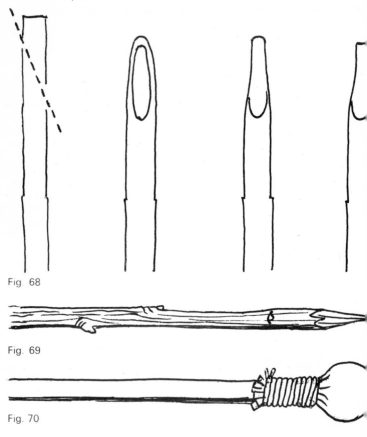

Fig. 68

Fig. 69

Fig. 70

Stick pens are exactly what they imply, and any quarter-inch thick twig will do to make one. Simply point it with a penknife. If no twigs are available, a sliver of fire-wood of the same thickness will do. In the same way as before, sharpen one end, dip in the ink, and draw.

Quill pens are slightly more difficult to make, but should be cut in the same way as the reed, with a sharp knife or razor-blade.

Mop pen: a small ball of cotton wool (absorbent cotton) is wrapped round with cloth and tied in a ball at the end of a stick (in the same way as a signwriter's mahl-stick is made). See fig. 70.

All the implements described and listed in this chapter have their own particular characteristics and produce their own kind of line. Try them out. You may never use any of them again, but you should experience what they can do, and what they can give you in terms of drawing and expressive line, singly or in combination. Who knows what you may discover.

Fig. 71

5 Inks and papers

There is a considerable variety of inks on the market these days. They fall into two main classes: waterproof inks and washable inks.

Waterproof inks are invaluable if you wish to float a wash over your drawing when it is finished. It would be difficult, if not impossible, to do this over washable ink, because the water would wash away the line, or at least blur it. It is possible to obtain a wide range of colours in both waterproof and washable inks. They are made up in bottles of various sizes, from one fluid ounce to as large as half-gallon containers. They are stocked by most stationers and artists' colourmen.

Sepia ink was at one time made from cuttle fish, but is now made synthetically. It is a neutral brown ink. The cuttle fish variety was much used by eighteenth and early nineteenth-century artists for landscape and figure drawing.

Chinese ink is made from carbon. It is a powerful black ink specially suitable for making drawings for reproduction as line blocks.

White, gold and silver inks are also available.

A useful home-made ink can be made from an ordinary domestic dye powder by mixing it with water. One powder to half a pint is a good proportion. Half a pint of ink will cost about ninepence, and will last a long time. Ink made in this way is particularly suitable for use with reed and bamboo pens, felt-tipped pens, stick pens, and mop pens.

Papers

Paper is expensive. Most watercolour papers are very expensive, some in the region of three shillings per imperial sheet. Cartridge (drawing) paper is also expensive, and so are sketch books made from watercolour or cartridge paper. To be productive study must go on all the time, so it is necessary to find a source of paper which will not be too dear. One good idea is to buy 'bank' paper (a thin paper with a smooth surface) which can be obtained from any stationer. Foolscap (legal) size is a practical format. You can get a ream of foolscap 'bank' for a very reasonable price, and this will enable you to make nearly five hundred sizeable drawings. A piece of hardboard, say 12″ × 8″, a bull-dog clip and wads of 'bank' make an inexpensive and practical solution to the problem of paper and sketch book.

For larger scale work a useful and not very expensive paper is decorators' lining paper. It can be cut into convenient sized sheets and used on a drawing board in the normal way. Cream sugar (construction) paper 18" wide can be bought in twelve-yard rolls.

The draftsman will want to keep a stock of good paper for ambitious work, for exhibitions and the rest. For this purpose cartridge (good quality drawing paper) is probably the best. It is possible to buy a quire of imperial size cartridge of medium weight for very little per sheet. Less expensive cartridge 30" wide can be bought in fifty-yard rolls.

Other papers readily available are:

Sugar (construction) paper 20" × 25" neutral colours

Brushwork paper $23\frac{1}{2}$" × 20" white and most colours

Watercolour papers David Cox and Ingres, Fabriano, d'Arches, Arnold

These watercolour papers represent only a few famous brands. There are many more. They are expensive, but you should try them. All the main artists' suppliers will gladly send you catalogues of papers. A list of suppliers is given on page 103.

6 Finding a subject

In the remaining pages I propose to show you a series of drawings by draftsmen of differing ages and ability. I have selected them specially to show as great a variety in approach, medium, scale and motivation as possible. They are in fact very diverse, and yet they all possess one quality in common: they are all vital drawings because they were all produced as a result of direct personal experience.

A good many of the draftsmen were pupils of mine, which gave me the opportunity to discuss their drawings with them. The captions to the illustrations indicate something of what stimulated the work; they also describe the media and state the dimensions of the original.

You will note that there are very few conventional subjects, i.e., subjects produced as the result of working to a convention or formula. Avoid this. Rely on direct experience. Study the reproductions; then try to think yourself into the situation in which each drawing was produced. Note the unexpected nature of a lot of the examples. This unexpectedness, oddly enough, is a product of the 'normalness' of the subject matter: of seeing normal things 'anew' in terms of drawing. Subjects are all round you all the time. The art of finding them and using them for drawing is a matter of sensitivity to environment, to occasion, to what is happening on the paper, to the suggestiveness of objects. It is also a matter of thinking in terms of shapes and seeing shapes everywhere, of selecting landscape elements and relating them together as shapes. It is a matter of knowing about, looking for and finding textures, patterns, themes; and the most important element in all this is *you*. The textures, shapes and forms which appeal to you will be different from those which delight other artist-draftsmen. This difference is what makes your drawings unique.

I hope that study of the drawings which follow will start trains of thought and sow the seeds of ideas. They should start you searching, and finding, new, exciting, personal subject-matter for your drawings.

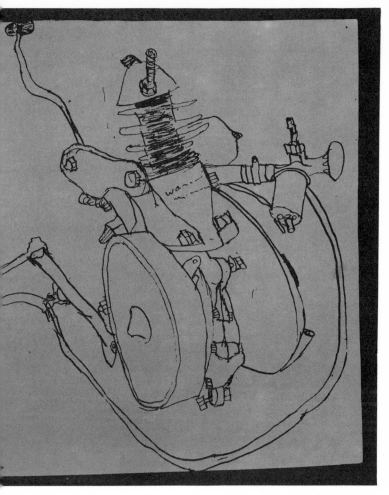

Fig. 72 *Study of a motorcycle engine* The young man who drew this was fascinated by the shapes to be found in machinery of all kinds; and this interest was coloured by his passion for motorcycles. The drawing is in steel-pen and waterproof ink on grey sugar (construction) paper. Size: $7\frac{1}{2}'' \times 6''$.

Figs. 73, 74 *Café de Flore, Paris* and *Rue de Buci, Paris* Two drawings in felt-tip pen. Some of the figures were drawn with a fountain pen. The drawings were part of a series based on the Paris scene. Size of both drawings: 14" × 10".

82

Fig. 75 *Madonna and child* A 'drawing' created by cutting the line in linoleum, then inking the linoleum and printing with it. The idea for this was sparked off by the need to produce a Christmas card and by an interest in the technique of lino-cutting.

Fig. 76 *Cwm Symlog, Cardiganshire* Drawn on medium tone paper. The lights were made by the addition of white ink, white chalk and white gouache; the darks by the use of black waterproof ink and black gouache. Size: 14" × 11".

Fig. 77

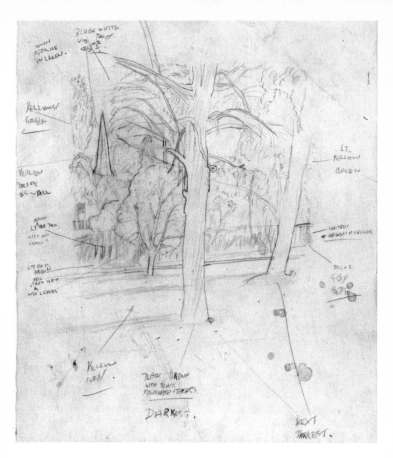

The annotations within the drawing read (approximately):

BLUISH WHITE TWIGS
WARM OPAQUE IN GREEN.
YELLOWISH GREEN
YELLOW BRIDGE & WALL
WARM LT GRN TRN. WITH OUT LEAVES
LT RK'D ABOVE YELL GREEN BRN WITH LEAVES
YELLOW GRN.
DARK BROWN WITH DARK PINKWRD STREAKS. DARKEST.
LT. YELLOW GREEN
WHITISH OR WARM YELLOW
PALE 2 GISH YELW
NEXT DARKEST.

Fig. 78 An annotated landscape drawing in pencil, made as a study for an oil painting. Size: 13″ × 10″.

Left:
Fig. 77 *Still-life drawing in silhouette* A study of the unexpected distortions of the shadows as compared with the objects; the whole treated as simple flat shapes. White pastel on dark buff paper. Objects and shadows were given equal importance and treated as simple shapes. Size: 14″ × 11″.

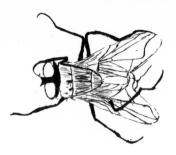

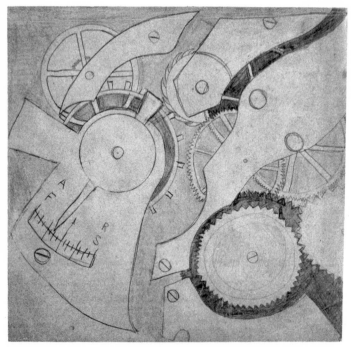

Fig. 79 Steel-pen drawing of a house-fly looked at through a magnifying glass. The ink was made from a black domestic dye-powder.
Fig. 80 Pencil drawing on medium grey paper of a watch interior, inspired by the beauty of the precision of watch shapes. Size: 14" × 14".

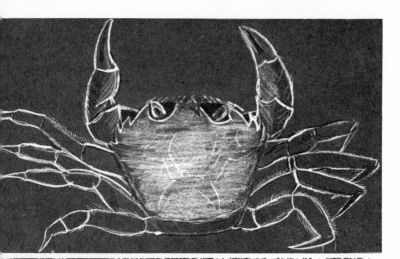

Fig. 81 Enlarged study of a crab drawn in white ink, white chalk and black ink on buff paper. Size: 10″ × 6″.

Fig. 82 *Hayrake* Drawn with felt-tip and fibre-tip pen on white paper. Size: 21″ × 16″.

Fig. 83 *Church at Auvers* This is the church that Van Gogh painted towards the end of his life. I wanted a personal souvenir of Auvers and its association with the famous Post-Impressionist painter. The drawing was made with a ball-point pen on white cartridge paper. Size: 14″ × 9″.

Fig. 84 *Tree shapes* A first attempt by an adult student, drawing with a felt-tipped pen on white cartridge paper and using the principle described in the first section of this book. This student was seeing and being inspired by 'shapes'. Size: 9″ × 6″.

Fig. 85 *Welsh Woodland* A free and powerful drawing in felt-tipped pen. A good example of the representation of solid form in line. The motivating factor was the power and virility of the tree-trunks. Size: 14″ × 10″.

Fig. 86 *Portrait heads* Drawn on bank paper with a Pentel fibre-tipped pen while watching television. It was an experiment to see whether it is possible to work from the TV screen.

Fig. 87 *Two studies of thumb prints* Above: brush and black ink on white cartridge paper. Size: 8" × 7½". Below: white chalk on black paper. Size: 11" × 7½". Both these drawings are drawings of textures produced by making an actual thumb print, studying this through a magnifying glass and then using a small viewfinder. Motive: visual exploration.

Fig. 88 *Study of bird in a cage* White ink on blue paper. To the artist the impelling feature was the pattern produced by the wires of the cage. Size: 4″ × 2½″.

Fig. 89 *The Farm in the trees* This watercolour drawing is a brief colour note of a Welsh farmyard. It is one of a series of colour studies made in preparation for a painting in oils. It was made on Whatman 'not' surface watercolour paper. Size: 11″ × 5″.

Fig. 90 *Undergrowth* Detail drawing inspired by a study of Douanier Rousseau. Made with ink and a cow-parsley stem, the background filled in with brush and ink. This very intricate drawing proved too much for the artist's patience, and it was never finished. Size: 25" × 10".

Overleaf: Two drawings in line, wash and wax resist. Fig. 91 Subject suggested by objects found on the beach developed as fantasy. Fig. 92 More realistic treatment of similar beach forms, with emphasis on textures. Deliberate use of beach forms to generate romantic imagery. Size of both: 7″ × 5″.

Fig. 91

Fig. 92

96

Fig. 93 *Design doodle* Made with compass and freehand line in pencil on pale blue paper. Geometry and automatic drawing. Size: 8″ × 6″.
Fig. 94 *Freehand doodles* Pen and black ink on white paper. Inspiration drawn from what was happening on the paper. Size: 5½″ × 5″

97

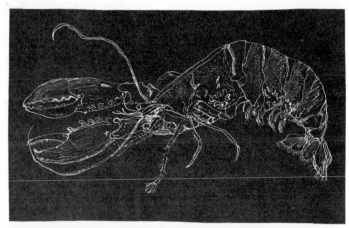

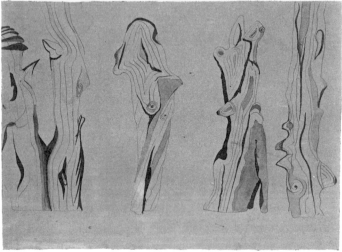

Fig. 95 *Lobster* Pen and white ink on black paper. Study in shape and texture. Size: 14" × 8".

Fig. 96 *Sea-defences* A drawing in steel pen produced after studying sea-eroded stumps of wood in a breakwater on the beach. These often assume strange forms and seem to take on grotesque personalities. It is a short step from these into a world of fantasy. Size: 22" × 15".

Fig. 97 *Welsh Stream* The white tree-trunks were produced by drawing them with a white wax candle on white paper and then brushing a wash of middle tone over. The wax repels the wash and the paper remains white. This is called wax-resist. The other drawing tools used were a watercolour brush and a twig pen. The composition of the drawing was inspired by the pattern of the shapes and contrasting tones of the rocks. Size: 30″ × 22″.

Fig. 98 *Llandre* A typical working study for an oil painting; roughly 'squared up' to aid translation to a large canvas of equal proportions. Ball-point and felt-tipped pen on white cartridge (drawing) paper. Size: 28″ × 12″.

It is comparatively easy to compose a drawing on a small scale. The eye controls the balance and harmony of a small drawing much more readily than that of a large work, say a canvas five feet by three feet. Without 'squaring' it is surprising how unexpectedly the proportions go adrift when a large version is being made from the original study. But if you square up, in inches, on a small sheet, say five inches by three inches, and then square up a large canvas with the same number and arrangement of squares, you will have a clear guide and the composition will approximate closely to your original sketch.

Fig. 99 *Study of tree-trunk* Hog-hair (bristle) brush and sepia watercolour on grey sugar (construction) paper. Emphasis on solidity. One of a series of studies of tree forms. Size: 30″ × 22″.

Conclusion

The main purpose of this book was stated in chapter one. It is to persuade readers that there are ways of beginning to draw which are genuinely within the capabilities of the many people who would like to draw but don't know how to begin. Another important aim is to encourage readers to train themselves, by study, to see.

With these two aims in mind, I have been urging the reader to look outwards, to study his environment objectively, to explore it and analyse it. Preoccupation with these two aims means that emphasis has been placed upon drawing from observation and composition from things seen. The only exceptions to this are the section on automatic drawing and the captions and illustrations in figs. 91, 92, 93, 94.

It is true that in order to draw we must first train the eye, then develop co-ordination of eye and hand, but we must remember that 'copying' is not the same thing as 'creating'. Imitation leaves little room for imagination or invention. None of the great masterpieces of art are mere copies or imitations of nature; they are transcriptions of experience, projections of vision, interpretations of reality, employing selection and accentuation of one or more of the many elements of experience. And these will not be only visual, tangible, or auditory, they may be emotional, spiritual or imaginary. I am not advocating only, or even mainly, the practice of representational drawing, nor do I think that creative work of pure fantasy and imagination is less significant. It is probably true to say that there are many more 'transcribers' than 'creators'; it is certainly true to say that it is a logical step from perceptive study to imaginative creativity.

It is possible to help the student by suggesting ways in which he can begin. The skill of drawing can be taught, and it is possible to assist the student to select appropriate areas of study. More than that the teacher cannot do. Beyond that you must go on alone. If your studies, explorations and discoveries in the realm of drawing involve you in stirring and vital experiences, then you will not be satisfied with representing only the observable super-ficialities of your subject. You will need to express something of your feelings as well.

From that moment your work will become creative expression, and you will be on your way towards maturity as an artist.

List of suppliers

George Rowney & Co. Ltd, 10/11 Percy Street, London, W.1.

Rowney (Canada) Ltd, 1021 Finch Avenue West, Downsview, Ontario.

The Morrilla Company of California, 2866 West 7th Street, Los Angles, California.

The Morilla Company, Inc., 43-01 21st Street, Long Island City, New York 11101.

Stafford-Reeves, Inc., 626, Greenwich Street, New York, 14.

Reeves and Sons Ltd, 13 Charing Cross Road, London, W.C.2.

Reeves and Sons (Canada) Ltd, 16 Apex Road, Toronto.

Reeves and Sons (Canada) Ltd, 519 West Pender Street, Vancouver, B.C.

M. Grumbacher Inc., 460 West 34 Street, New York.

F. Weber Co., Wayne and Windrim Streets, Philadelphia 19144, Pa.

Winsor and Newton Ltd, 51 Rathbone Place, London, W.1.

Winsor and Newton Inc, 881 Broadway, New York.

Suppliers are always ready to answer queries. Many of them publish pocket-size catalogues which they will send on request. Such catalogues contain, as well as lists of materials, the addresses of local dealers.

In America you can write to large art supply dealers for catalogs. Arthur Brown, 2 West 46 Street, New York, N.Y. 10036, and A. I. Friedman, 25 West 45 Street, New York, N.Y. 10036, are two major American suppliers.

Index